QUILTING PATTERNS

110 Ready-to-Use Machine Quilting Designs

Linda Macho

Dover Publications, Inc.
Mineola, New York

Dedication

To my parents, Robert and Evelyn,
who encouraged me to explore the joy of creativity;
to my brothers, Jim, Richard and Jerry,
who have always appreciated the finished projects;
and to my sister, Danae,
who puts up with needles in the carpet and typing late at night.

Bibliographical Note

Quilting Patterns: 110 Ready-to-Use Machine Quilting Designs is a republication of the work *Quilting Patterns: 110 Full-Size Ready-to-Use Designs and Complete Instructions*, originally printed by Dover Publications, Inc., Mineola, New York, in 1984.

Instructional diagrams by Janette Aiello
Book design by Barbara Effron

Library of Congress Cataloging-in-Publication Data

Names: Macho, Linda, 1955– author.
Title: Quilting patterns : 110 ready-to-use machine quilting designs / Linda Macho.
Description: Mineola, New York : Dover Publications, Inc., [2019] | "Quilting Patterns: 110 Ready-to-Use Machine Quilting Designs is an unabridged republication of the work Quilting Patterns: 110 Full-Size Ready-to-Use Designs and Complete Instructions, originally printed by Dover Publications, Inc., Mineola, New York, in 1984"— Title verso.
Identifiers: LCCN 2019016773 | ISBN 9780486838151 | ISBN 0486838153
Subjects: LCSH: Machine quilting—Patterns. | Quilting—Patterns.
Classification: LCC TT835 .M27 2019 | DDC 746.46/041—dc23
LC record available at https://lccn.loc.gov/2019016773

Manufactured in the United States by LSC Communications
83815301
www.doverpublications.com

2 4 6 8 10 9 7 5 3 1

2019

Introduction

Quilting is addictive. It is not the kind of addiction that will result in bodily harm (except, perhaps, sore fingertips), but it is the kind of addiction that creates an unquenchable thirst for new patterns, fabrics, notions and books. And this addiction, when well fueled by the items just mentioned, will release creative impulses and liberate previously hidden talents. The process of selecting a pattern, picking a color scheme, deciding upon fabrics, cutting, sewing and quilting is one of the best methods of relaxation available today, as it was in the past. Quilting is a completely satisfying form of needlework because it combines so many skills and talents that meld to create a useful and cherished work.

There is a tremendous wealth of information on quilting in the many books currently available in needlework stores, quilt shops, bookstores and libraries. You can obtain books on the history of quilting, how to appliqué and how to make a patchwork quilt, as well as collections of patchwork patterns and volumes showing finished quilts and related projects. Some of these books touch upon the actual technique of quilting (securing the three layers of the quilt "sandwich"—top, batting and backing—with a running stitch), but none of these books is devoted solely to "how to quilt." This book is a comprehensive guide to the technique of quilting, and contains all the information you'll need to learn how to quilt and how to use the 110 quilting patterns included in the volume.

After you have learned how to use your patterns, transfer your markings, place the quilt sandwich in a frame or hoop and work those rhythmic running stitches, you can select several of the traditional quilting designs in the template section of this book and really get to work. Then, if you decide that you want to know the history of quilting, or how to make a patchwork quilt top or appliqué a design, you can choose some of the books from the Selected Bibliography on page 14.

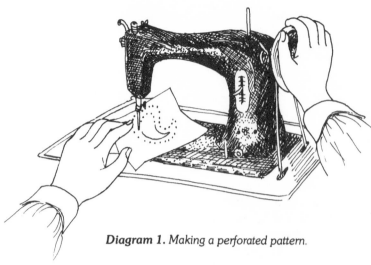

Diagram 1. *Making a perforated pattern.*

Diagram 2. *Rubbing powder through the holes of a perforated pattern to transfer the design.*

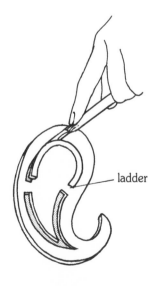

ladder

Diagram 3. *Cutting channels in a quilting stencil.*

How to Use the Patterns

There are 110 traditional and contemporary quilting patterns (plates 1 to 32) printed at the back of this book. These patterns can be used alone or in combination with one another. Just as there are many ways of using the designs, there are several methods for preparing the patterns and transferring them to your fabric. Four methods are described here.

Making a Perforated Pattern

For this method you will need scissors, a sewing machine, fine sandpaper, French chalk or cornstarch (for dark fabrics), cocoa, cinnamon or snuff (for light fabrics) and a No. 2 pencil.

Cut out the desired pattern, leaving at least ¼" to ½" of blank paper all around. Remove the pressure foot from your sewing machine and place the pattern directly beneath the needle. Set your stitch length for 6-stitches-per-inch. Begin "sewing" very slowly by turning the wheel to raise and lower the needle while carefully guiding the pattern so the needle pierces the paper along the design lines *(Diagram 1)*. Continue until your entire design has been pierced in this manner. The patterns can also be perforated by using a pushpin, tiny nail or another sharp instrument; keep the perforations even and centered exactly over the lines.

Remove the paper from the sewing machine and gently sand the wrong side to open up the holes completely and remove excess paper that may be protruding from the wrong side. Then, pin the pattern to your fabric and rub powder through the holes with a cotton ball or soft cloth *(Diagram 2)*. If the fabric is dark, use French chalk or cornstarch; if the fabric is light, use cocoa, cinnamon, snuff or another dark powder. Carefully remove the pattern from the fabric without disturbing the powder. Go over all of the powdered design lines with a lead pencil to make them permanent enough to last through the quilting process. Then, shake or brush away the powder.

Making a Quilting Stencil

For this method you will need scissors, illustration board or heavy cardboard, rubber cement, an X-ACTO knife, fine sandpaper and a No. 2 pencil (for light fabrics) or an artist's white chalk or pencil (for dark fabrics).

Cut out the desired pattern, leaving at least ¼" of blank paper all around. Using rubber cement, glue the pattern onto illustration board or cardboard. Allow the glue to dry, then, using an X-ACTO knife, carefully cut out the pattern along the lines of the design.

For simple quilting patterns with interior spaces, either cut out the spaces using an X-ACTO knife or cut channels in the template along the lines that must be transferred *(Diagram 3);* "ladders" must be left in the channels to allow interior spaces to remain attached to the template. The channels must be wide enough to accommodate your sharpened pencil point. For complicated interior lines, such as on the feather patterns, cut channels for the major lines (the center line of the feather, for example) then draw the remainder of the pattern freehand after the outline of the template has been drawn on the fabric.

After all outlines, spaces and channels have been cut, carefully sand all rough edges of the stencil with fine sandpaper, making the illustration board or cardboard align perfectly with the lines on the quilting pattern.

Position the quilting stencil on your fabric and trace lightly along the edges with a well-sharpened lead pencil or white artist's chalk or pencil—depending upon the color of the fabric you are marking. After the outline has been transferred, trace along each channel or interior space to transfer inner design lines. Draw in any extra design lines after the pattern has been removed.

A quilting stencil can also be made from clear plastic or Mylar. This plastic may be found in art-supply stores or quilt shops.

To make a plastic stencil, position the plastic over the pattern and trace all the design lines using a marking pen or a ball-point pen or stylus that will leave an impression on the plastic. Carefully cut channels for the design lines using an X-ACTO knife. Position the stencil over your fabric and carefully mark the design as shown in *Diagram 4.*

Two Other Methods for Using the Patterns

The quilting designs can be traced onto tracing paper or Mylar and transferred to your fabric using a tracing wheel and dressmaker's carbon paper. After tracing the design, pin the Mylar or tracing paper to your fabric, leaving two edges free. Slip dressmaker's carbon paper (white or yellow for dark fabrics; red, blue or yellow for light fabrics) face down between the pattern and the fabric. Do not pin the carbon because the pins will leave marks. Carefully go over all of the lines with a tracing wheel *(Diagram 5);* use a wheel with "teeth" that will leave a dotted line.

Another method can also be used. It is called "needle-marking" and is used primarily by quilters who do not mark the entire quilt top at one time, but who mark individual designs as they go along. This marking is done after the quilt top, batting and backing have been assembled and the quilt is already in the frame.

Cut out the desired pattern and carefully trim away excess paper close to the edge of the design. Position the pattern on the quilt top and trace around the edge with a blunt needle such as a large thick yarn needle, leaving a crease mark on the fabric. This method is also called "scratching" but the material should not actually be scratched; the needle should be held at a sharp angle and pressed firmly into the fabric *(Diagram 6).* One can then quilt along the clearly defined indentations made with the needle.

Diagram 4. Using a plastic stencil to mark a quilting design.

Diagram 5. Using a tracing wheel and dressmaker's carbon to transfer a quilting design.

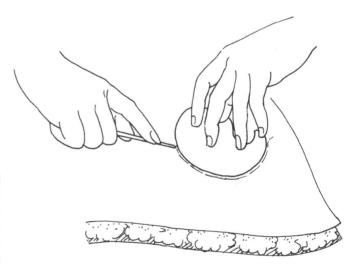

Diagram 6. Needle-marking a quilting design.

Quilting Equipment

Needles

Quilting needles can be purchased in sizes 7–10; these needles are also called "betweens." The higher the number, the smaller the needle. The tightness of the weave, the size of your hand and the thickness of the batting will dictate the best needle size for you. The average needle is size 8.

Basting Thread

Any strong thread that will hold up to the stress of the frame or hoop is acceptable. Try to use a light-colored thread that will contrast with your fabric and quilting thread; this will make it easier to find and remove your basting thread after you have finished quilting. Do not use dark thread which may leave shadows after the basting is removed.

Quilting Thread

100% cotton quilting thread should be used. There are several brands and a wide range of colors from which to choose. You must decide how much you want your quilting stitches to show; for most projects, it is the indentation formed by the stitches that gives textural interest to the quilt—not the quilting stitches themselves—so select a quilting thread that will blend inconspicuously into your background fabric.

Tape Measure

This will be needed when marking placements for specific quilting motifs.

Scissors

Use one pair of household scissors for cutting the paper patterns; use a pair of very sharp scissors when quilting to clip threads—small embroidery scissors work well.

Large Safety Pins

These are used to initially hold the three layers of the quilt together before basting.

Iron

The quilt top and lining must be perfectly ironed before assembly; a steam iron would best accomplish this.

Batting

Cotton batting is available in sheets in several sizes; it must be handled with care and the quilting stitches must be closely worked to prevent shifting and bunching. *Dacron polyester battings* are widely used because of their washability, ease in handling and wide availability in many sizes and thicknesses. Because the polyester batting will not shift or bunch easily, larger areas can be left unquilted, allowing more freedom in designing, and lessening the amount of time needed to finish the quilt. *Wool batting* combines qualities of cotton and polyester batting. It must be closely quilted like cotton batting, but it will achieve the loft of polyester batting, creating a strongly defined pattern on the quilt top.

Beeswax or Paraffin

Thread should be waxed when hand-quilting to strengthen the thread and prevent it from knotting. Waxing the thread will also allow it to slide smoothly through the quilt layers.

Thimbles

Use a flat-faced metal thimble rather than one with a rounded end. The thimble should fit snugly on the middle finger of your sewing hand. Two thimbles may also be used. Right-handed quilters should place one thimble on the middle finger of the right hand and one on the index finger of the left hand. Left-handed quilters should use a thimble on the middle finger of the left hand and one on the index finger of the right hand.

Quilting Frames and Hoops

The purpose of using a quilting frame or hoop is to maintain an easy, even tension on the three layers of the quilt sandwich—the backing, batting and top—keeping the layers from sagging or shifting and enabling you to quilt evenly. The selection of a quilting frame or hoop is a matter of individual choice. There are advantages and disadvantages to using either one, and some quilters prefer not using one at all (although this is not recommended). Basically the decision of what type of frame to use is based on the amount of space available and where you want to quilt. Full frames allow even tension on the quilt layers at all times, but take up a great deal of room. Hoops are more versatile, enabling you to quilt in various places if you wish, but great care must be taken initially to prevent the layers of the quilt sandwich from shifting. Following is a discussion of the various types of frames and hoops available, and how to set up a quilt in each.

Full Frame

Made out of lengths of wood slightly larger than the entire quilt, a full frame was very popular when quilting bees were common, because a large number of women were able to quilt at the same time.

To work with a full frame, assemble four wooden strips (each slightly larger than the size of the finished quilt top) into a rectangular (or even a square) shape using C-clamps. Cut strips of sturdy fabric the length of each strip of wood and about 4″ wide for the fabric "aprons." Staple the aprons to the strips of wood with the excess fabric facing the center of the rectangle. Pin or sew the quilt back, wrong side up, to the aprons to keep it quite taut. Next, spread the batting evenly over the backing. Place the quilt top, right side up, over the batting. Pin or baste the three layers together, then place the frame on legs or the backs of chairs. Quilting on a full frame should start at the edges, working toward the center. As the outer edges are completed, the quilted portions are rolled around two opposite strips of the frame and the C-clamps are adjusted, enabling the quilters to reach the center area. Great care must be taken to keep the tension of the quilt layers even at all times to prevent a bubble from forming in the center.

Several quilters who prefer using the full frame have solved the space problem by attaching the frame to a rope and pulley system. When they are through quilting for the day, the frame is hoisted to the ceiling where it remains suspended until the next quilting session!

Roller Frame

Roller frames consist of two wooden bars the width of the quilt (the rollers) and two cross-pieces that hold the rollers in place to keep the quilt taut (the stretchers). Sturdy fabric aprons are attached to the rollers, and the quilt sandwich is attached to each apron and rolled until

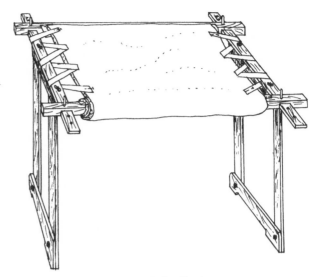

Diagram 7. A roller frame.

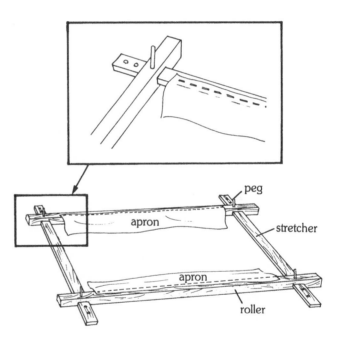

Diagram 8. A close look at a roller frame.

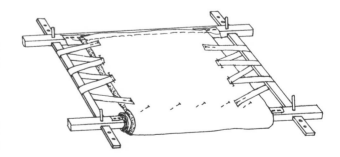

Diagram 9. Attaching the quilt to the stretchers with fabric strips.

it is taut. The frame must be supported by legs or chair backs at the four corners (Diagram 7).

There are two schools of thought as to how long the stretchers should be. Some quilters say that the stretchers should be equal to one arm-length because they feel that the quilting should proceed in one direction only. This will make the quilting process slightly more time-consuming in that more rollings will be required. Also, many quilters prefer to work from both sides of the frame, particularly when working intricate curves that make quilting in one direction awkward. The other concept is to make the stretchers approximately two arm-lengths so a quilter can reach to the center of the quilt from each side of the frame, reducing the number of rollings.

Regardless of the length of the stretchers, all bars should be made of a smooth, hard wood with a hole $\frac{1}{2}''$ in diameter at each end of each bar. When the bars are assembled they are held in place with wooden or metal pegs fitted into the holes (Diagram 8).

To set up a quilt in a roller frame, assemble the quilt back, batting and top; see page 9 for assembly instructions. Attach each end of the quilt to the frame by sewing all three layers to the apron on each roller; roll the ends of the quilt evenly onto each roller until the quilt is held taut between them. Using bias tape or fabric strips about 1″ wide, wind and pin the tape to the sides of the quilt and to the stretchers as shown in Diagram 9, keeping an even tension across the quilt. The quilting can now proceed. When the exposed area has been fully quilted, remove the bias tape and roll the quilted portion out of the way, exposing a fresh area; reattach the bias tape. Continue in this manner until the quilt top is finished.

A roller frame does not take up as much space as a full frame, yet it has many of the advantages of a full frame in that it will hold the quilt under even tension, and it is large enough for several people to quilt comfortably. Also, the rollers provide a resting place for tired arms, and quilting thread, needles and scissors can sit within easy reach on the unrolled surface.

Quilt-As-You-Go Frame

This frame is used by those who prefer to quilt one block at a time; the quilt blocks are later assembled to form the complete quilt. Quilt-as-you-go frames, available in adjustable sizes, are simply four strips of wood secured at the corners with wing nuts. Fabric aprons are stapled to the wood strips and the quilt block (consisting of backing, batting and top) is sewn or pinned to the fabric aprons to keep it taut. Usually, little or no basting is required for this method. The frame can be held in the lap or secured to a stand while quilting.

The disadvantage to this rather convenient method of quilting is that the quilt must obviously be assembled in blocks. Also, the quilting design must not come closer than $\frac{1}{4}''$ from the edge of the block because there must be sufficient free fabric to join the blocks at the edges. Joining the blocks is a tedious process which entails stitching the quilted tops together, whip-stitching the edges of the batting together, then lapping and hand-sewing the backing in place. However, the saving of time in the actual quilting and the convenience of this method may more than make up for the time it will take to assemble the blocks.

Quilting Hoop

A round wooden quilting hoop about 24″ in diameter is an excellent alternative to a full or roller frame. It is portable yet provides a working area large enough to prevent frequent repositioning. Wooden hoops should have an adjustable outer frame; this usually consists of wooden blocks through which a bolt is tightened. It is a good idea to wrap the hoop with muslin to protect the quilt from whatever acids may be present in the wood. Hoops can be attached to a stand or can be supported against a table or chair while quilting. The quilt sandwich must be thoroughly basted if the work is to be quilted in a hoop. If the quilt is sufficiently basted, however, the results can be compared quite favorably to those achieved when using a frame.

Assembling the Quilt Sandwich

Once the quilt top is completed and ready for quilting, the quilt sandwich must be assembled. First, carefully iron the backing and the quilt top. This is the last time these fabrics will ever be ironed so take your time and remove every wrinkle! If using a full frame, refer to the assembly instructions on page 7. If using a roller frame or hoop, spread the backing, wrong side up, on a large flat surface (usually an uncovered floor is the best place —if possible, take up the rug to prevent pinning your quilt layers to it). Spread your batting evenly over the backing; this job is relatively easy if using polyester batting. If using cotton or wool batting, spread it *carefully* over the backing using the utmost caution to prevent holes or thin spots from forming. It is an extra step, but basting the batting to the backing will ensure smooth, even coverage with no shifting once the quilt top is put in place; the basting stitches needn't be close—just take long anchoring stitches across the length and width of the batting and backing.

Once the batting is smoothly in place, carefully lay your quilt top right side up, over the batting. Smooth and ease the quilt top so it fits squarely and evenly over the other two layers. Using large safety pins, secure the three layers starting from the center and working out toward the sides and corners; use as many pins as you feel are necessary to keep the layers from shifting. Next, thoroughly baste the three layers together following *Diagram 10*. Use a long strand of basting thread, knotted at the end. Start in the center and work outward toward the edges of the quilt diagonally, horizontally and vertically. The stitches can be quite long, but you must keep two things in mind at all times while basting. First, the basting stitches must secure all three layers of the quilt sandwich. Second, the backing must be kept completely smooth at all times; check constantly (by feel) for any pulls or wrinkles in the backing and correct them immediately. If you take your time in the basting process, you can practically be assured of superb results in the quilting process. If using a hoop, it is recommended that you baste between the other lines as shown in *Diagram 11*. This is not necessary if you are using a roller frame.

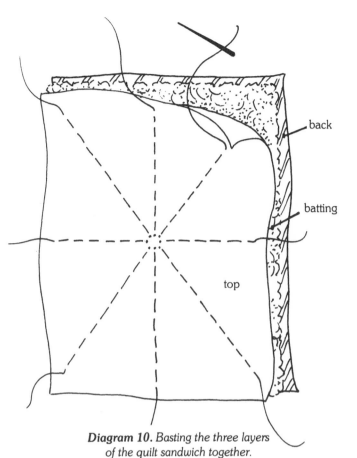

Diagram 10. Basting the three layers of the quilt sandwich together.

Diagram 11. Additional basting—recommended if using a quilting hoop.

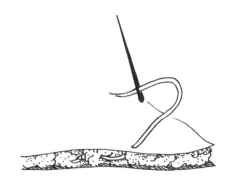

Diagram 12. Starting a quilting thread—insert the needle only through the top and the batting.

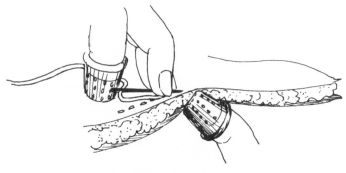

Diagram 13. Burying the knot in the batting.

How to Quilt

While neatness and precision are essential, the most important aspect of quilting is rhythm. Rhythm will not only make quilting more relaxing and enjoyable, but it will contribute toward making your stitches neat and even. The best way to achieve this rhythm is to sit comfortably in front of your frame with your sewing hand on top of the quilt and the other hand below—ready to guide the needle in its up-and-down motion. Use a thimble on the middle finger of your sewing hand or on each hand; see page 6 for directions on how to wear two thimbles. The diagrams in this section illustrate the use of two thimbles. Remember that every quilting stitch must go through all three layers of the quilt sandwich and the stitches (and the space between them) should have the same appearance on each side of the quilt.

Use one strand of thread in your quilting needle. Make a small knot at the end of the thread and insert the needle through the top and batting only *(Diagram 12)*. Tug the thread until the knot pops below the surface of the quilt top to be buried in the batting *(Diagram 13)*. Some quilters prefer to have several working needles going at the same time, especially when quilting a border or filling. If several needles are in use at the same time, the work can advance evenly across the quilt. This, however, is a matter of personal choice.

Diagram 14. The quilting stitch—guide the needle through the surface until it makes contact with the thimble below the quilt.

Diagram 15. Pressing against the quilt with your thumb to "help" the needle back to the surface.

Quilting stitches are actually running stitches. With the threaded end of the needle resting against the thimble on the hand above the quilt, guide the needle at a slight angle into the quilt's surface so the point of the needle makes contact with the index finger or the thimble on the hand below the quilt *(Diagram 14)*. The finger or thimble below the quilt should be exerting enough pressure to cause a ridge in the surface, enabling you to determine exactly where to aim the point of the needle. As the needle touches the finger or thimble below the quilt, direct it back to the surface of the quilt top and pull needle and thread through, completing the first stitch. The needle can be "helped" back to the surface by pressing against the quilt with your thumb *(Diagram 15)*; this will also aid in keeping the spaces between the stitches even.

When you are working on a patchwork quilt, there are times when the quilting stitches must cross seamlines. It is difficult to work the running stitch across the extra thickness made by the seam allowances, so work two to four stab stitches across the difficult area *(Diagram 16)*, giving an extra tug to the thread with each of these stab stitches.

To end a line of quilting, make a small backstitch through the backing and batting, forming a loop as shown in *Diagram 17*. Pull the thread taut then make another stitch, drawing the needle through the batting for about 1". Pull needle and thread to the surface, hold taut and clip the thread close to the quilt top *(Diagram 18)*.

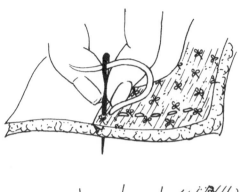

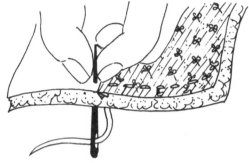

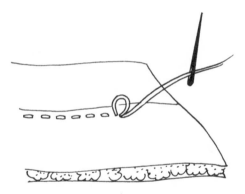

Diagram 16. Working stab stitches across a seam allowance.

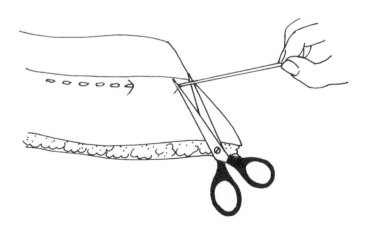

Diagram 17. Ending a line of quilting stitches with a backstitch.

Diagram 18. Clipping the end of the quilting thread.

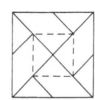

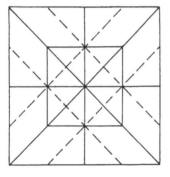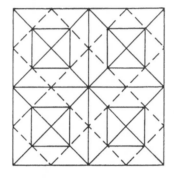

Diagram 19. *Examples of selective outline quilting.*

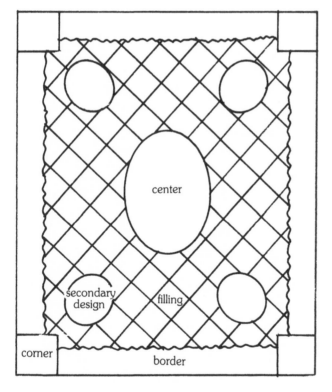

Diagram 20. *The basic components of a white-on-white quilt.*

How to Select Quilting Patterns

The selection of quilting patterns is the most challenging yet most creative aspect of quilting. Since the quilting stitches really are "the icing on the cake" (or should that be "the mayo on the sandwich"?), the selection of patterns should be made while the quilt top is being designed. The quilting designs must harmonize with the quilt top, enhancing the quilt in a subtle yet dramatic way. Much will depend upon whether the quilt top is made of patchwork, appliqué or a single layer of fabric to be embellished only with quilting.

Outline quilting is quite acceptable for patchwork and appliqué quilts. In essence, the fabric shapes are outlined with one or many rows of running stitches that echo the lines of the design. When outline-quilting a patchwork design, it is often more interesting to create secondary designs with your quilting by selectively outlining certain patches or by connecting the patches in an unusual way. See Diagram 19 for several examples of selective outline quilting.

Another popular form of quilting patchwork is to work filling or ground patterns across the entire quilt. Several filling patterns are illustrated on the facing page.

Quite often, patchwork quilts will be composed of patchwork blocks interspersed with solid blocks of fabric and this is where you can be quite creative with single quilting motifs, working an elaborate design in each blank block. What you must remember is that the quilting should not overwhelm the patchwork design but complement it, either by picking up a theme of the patchwork (baskets, pinwheels, flowers) or by contrasting with it (using a curvilinear quilting design with a geometric quilt top).

Designing a "white-on-white" quilt is a bit more complicated. These quilts contain five basic components; see Diagram 20. The most important component is the *center* of the quilt. This center can be composed of several different units that repeat or are reversed, creating a bold yet balanced round, oval or square unit. The *secondary designs* should carry out the theme of the center, filling in the spaces between the center and the border; the secondary designs are dispensable, however, and can be replaced with the *filling design* if a simpler quilt is desired. *Borders* and *corners* are the fourth and fifth elements. The corners can be distinct units that perhaps repeat one of the units in the center, or they can be a continuation of the border design. Use tracing paper to design your white-on-white quilt, selecting basic quilting elements from the pattern section in this book; combine, tilt, reverse or overlap these patterns to create a well-balanced and distinctive design. A white-on-white quilt is rather ambitious, so consider your skill level, time and patience when selecting the quilting patterns.

Filling Patterns

Selected Bibliography

BONESTEEL, GEORGIA. *Lap Quilting With Georgia Bonesteel.* Birmingham, Alabama: Oxmoor House, 1982.

COLBY, AVERIL. *Quilting.* New York: Charles Scribner's Sons, 1971.

CORWIN, JUDITH HOFFMAN. *Easy-to-Make Appliqué Quilts for Children.* New York: Dover Publications, Inc., 1982.

GUTCHEON, BETH. *The Perfect Patchwork Primer.* New York: Penguin Books, 1973.

HECHTLINGER, ADELAIDE. *American Quilts, Quilting, and Patchwork.* New York: A & W Publishers, 1974.

HINSON, DOLORES A. *Quilting Manual.* 1970. Reprint, New York: Dover Publications, Inc., 1980.

ICKIS, MARGUERITE. *The Standard Book of Quilt Making and Collecting.* 1949. Reprint, New York: Dover Publications, Inc., 1959.

JAMES, MICHAEL. *The Quiltmaker's Handbook.* Englewood Cliffs, New Jersey: Prentice-Hall, Inc., 1978.

LEMAN, BONNIE. *Quick and Easy Quilting.* Wheatridge, Colorado: Moon Over the Mountain Publishing Company, 1979.

McKIM, RUBY SHORT. *101 Patchwork Patterns.* 1931. Reprint, New York: Dover Publications, Inc., 1962.

MURWIN, SUSAN AYLSWORTH, and PAYNE, SUZZY CHALFANT. *Quick and Easy Patchwork on the Sewing Machine.* New York: Dover Publications, Inc., 1979.

ROSE, HELEN WHITSON. *Quilting With Strips and Strings.* New York: Dover Publications, Inc., 1983.

WEBSTER, MARIE D. *Quilts: Their Story and How to Make Them.* New York: Tudor Publishing Company, 1915.

Metric Conversion Chart

CONVERTING INCHES TO CENTIMETERS AND YARDS TO METERS

mm — millimeters   cm — centimeters   m — meters

INCHES INTO MILLIMETERS AND CENTIMETERS
(Slightly rounded off for convenience)

inches	mm		cm	inches	cm	inches	cm	inches	cm
⅛	3mm			5	12.5	21	53.5	38	96.5
¼	6mm			5½	14	22	56	39	99
⅜	10mm	or	1cm	6	15	23	58.5	40	101.5
½	13mm	or	1.3cm	7	18	24	61	41	104
⅝	15mm	or	1.5cm	8	20.5	25	63.5	42	106.5
¾	20mm	or	2cm	9	23	26	66	43	109
⅞	22mm	or	2.2cm	10	25.5	27	68.5	44	112
1	25mm	or	2.5cm	11	28	28	71	45	114.5
1¼	32mm	or	3.2cm	12	30.5	29	73.5	46	117
1½	38mm	or	3.8cm	13	33	30	76	47	119.5
1¾	45mm	or	4.5cm	14	35.5	31	79	48	122
2	50mm	or	5cm	15	38	32	81.5	49	124.5
2½	65mm	or	6.5cm	16	40.5	33	84	50	127
3	75mm	or	7.5cm	17	43	34	86.5		
3½	90mm	or	9cm	18	46	35	89		
4	100mm	or	10cm	19	48.5	36	91.5		
4½	115mm	or	11.5cm	20	51	37	94		

YARDS TO METERS
(Slightly rounded off for convenience)

yards	meters	yards	meters	yards	meters	yards	meters	yards	meters
⅛	0.15	2⅛	1.95	4⅛	3.80	6⅛	5.60	8⅛	7.45
¼	0.25	2¼	2.10	4¼	3.90	6¼	5.75	8¼	7.55
⅜	0.35	2⅜	2.20	4⅜	4.00	6⅜	5.85	8⅜	7.70
½	0.50	2½	2.30	4½	4.15	6½	5.95	8½	7.80
⅝	0.60	2⅝	2.40	4⅝	4.25	6⅝	6.10	8⅝	7.90
¾	0.70	2¾	2.55	4¾	4.35	6¾	6.20	8¾	8.00
⅞	0.80	2⅞	2.65	4⅞	4.50	6⅞	6.30	8⅞	8.15
1	0.95	3	2.75	5	4.60	7	6.40	9	8.25
1⅛	1.05	3⅛	2.90	5⅛	4.70	7⅛	6.55	9⅛	8.35
1¼	1.15	3¼	3.00	5¼	4.80	7¼	6.65	9¼	8.50
1⅜	1.30	3⅜	3.10	5⅜	4.95	7⅜	6.75	9⅜	8.60
1½	1.40	3½	3.20	5½	5.05	7½	6.90	9½	8.70
1⅝	1.50	3⅝	3.35	5⅝	5.15	7⅝	7.00	9⅝	8.80
1¾	1.60	3¾	3.45	5¾	5.30	7¾	7.10	9¾	8.95
1⅞	1.75	3⅞	3.55	5⅞	5.40	7⅞	7.20	9⅞	9.05
2	1.85	4	3.70	6	5.50	8	7.35	10	9.15

AVAILABLE FABRIC WIDTHS

25"	65cm	50"	127cm
27"	70cm	54"/56"	140cm
35"/36"	90cm	58"/60"	150cm
39"	100cm	68"/70"	175cm
44"/45"	115cm	72"	180cm
48"	122cm		

AVAILABLE ZIPPER LENGTHS

4"	10cm	10"	25cm	22"	55cm
5"	12cm	12"	30cm	24"	60cm
6"	15cm	14"	35cm	26"	65cm
7"	18cm	16"	40cm	28"	70cm
8"	20cm	18"	45cm	30"	75cm
9"	22cm	20"	50cm		

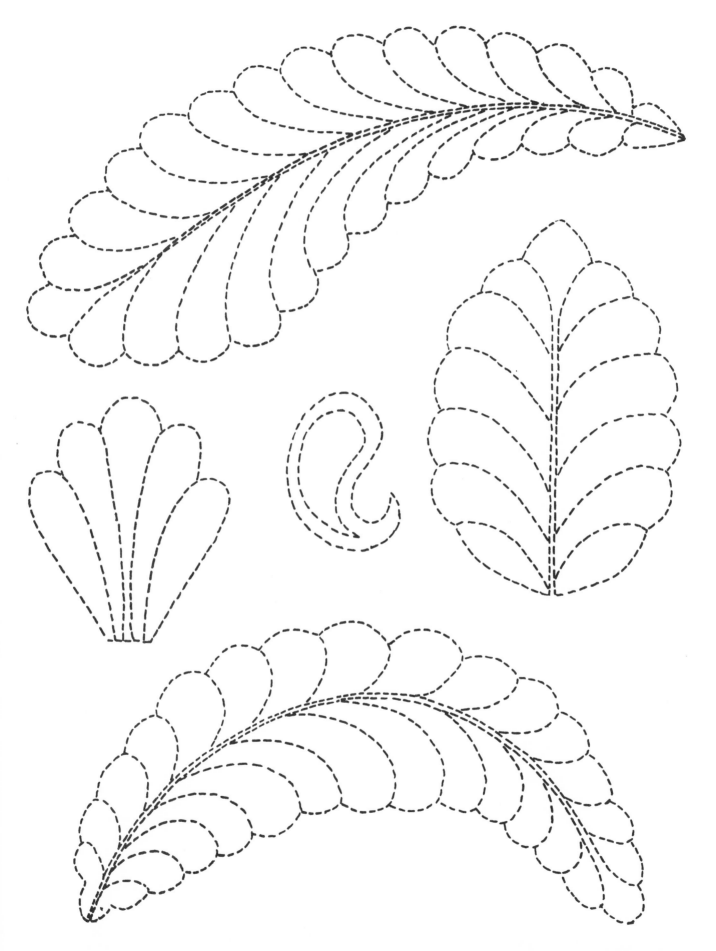

PLATE 1

PLATE 2

PLATE 3

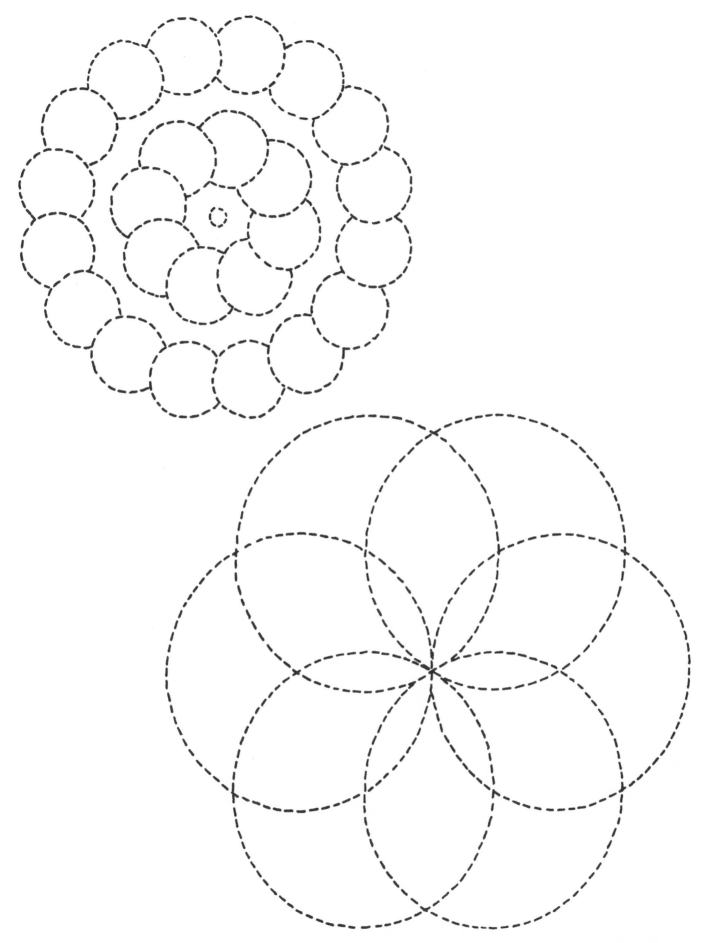

PLATE 4

PLATE 5

PLATE 6

PLATE 7

PLATE 8

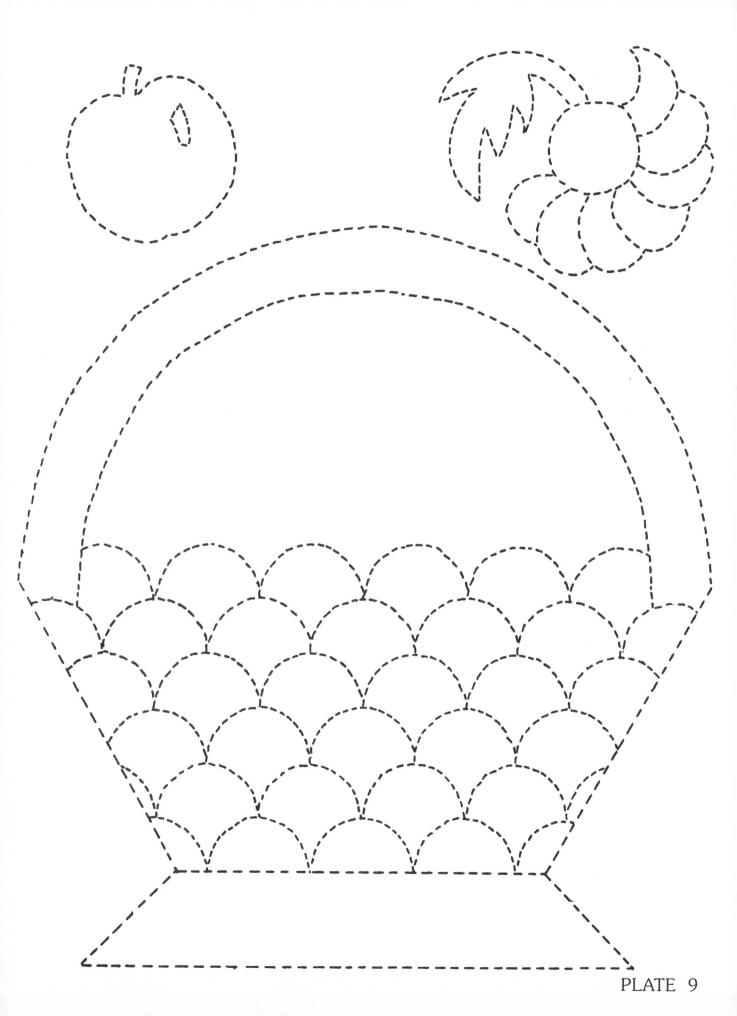

PLATE 9

PLATE 10

PLATE 11

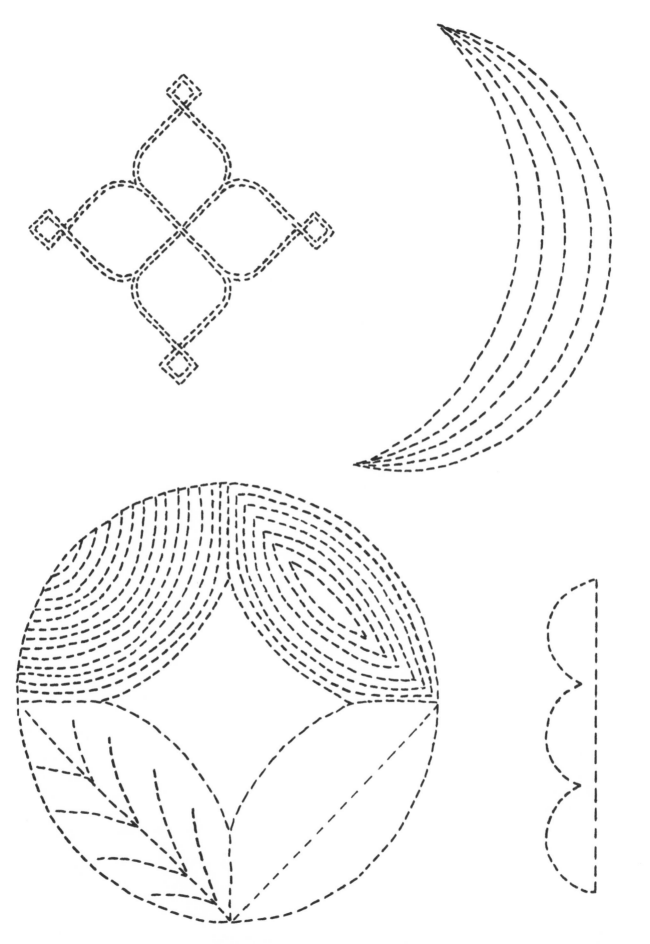

PLATE 12

PLATE 13

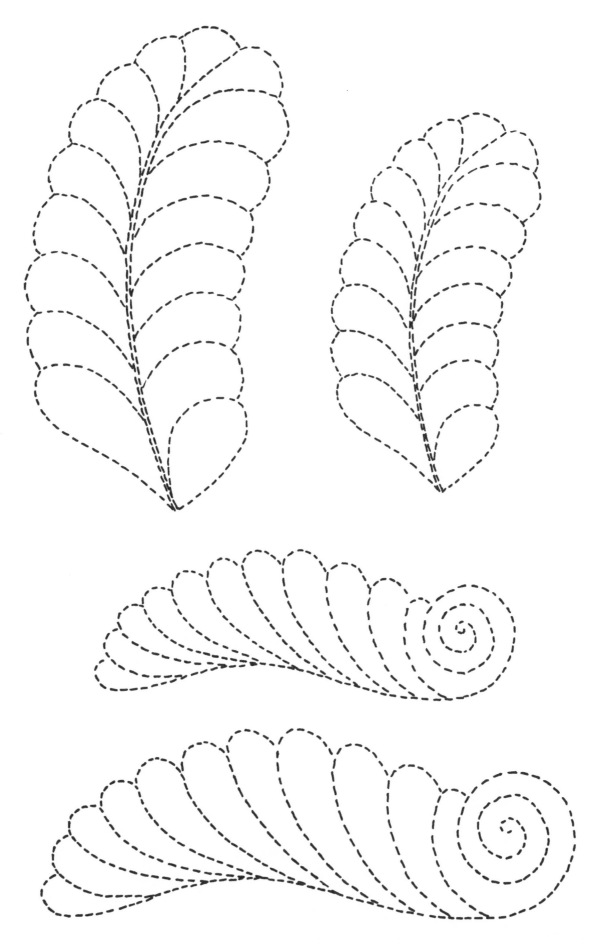

PLATE 14

PLATE 15

PLATE 16

PLATE 17

PLATE 18

PLATE 19

PLATE 20

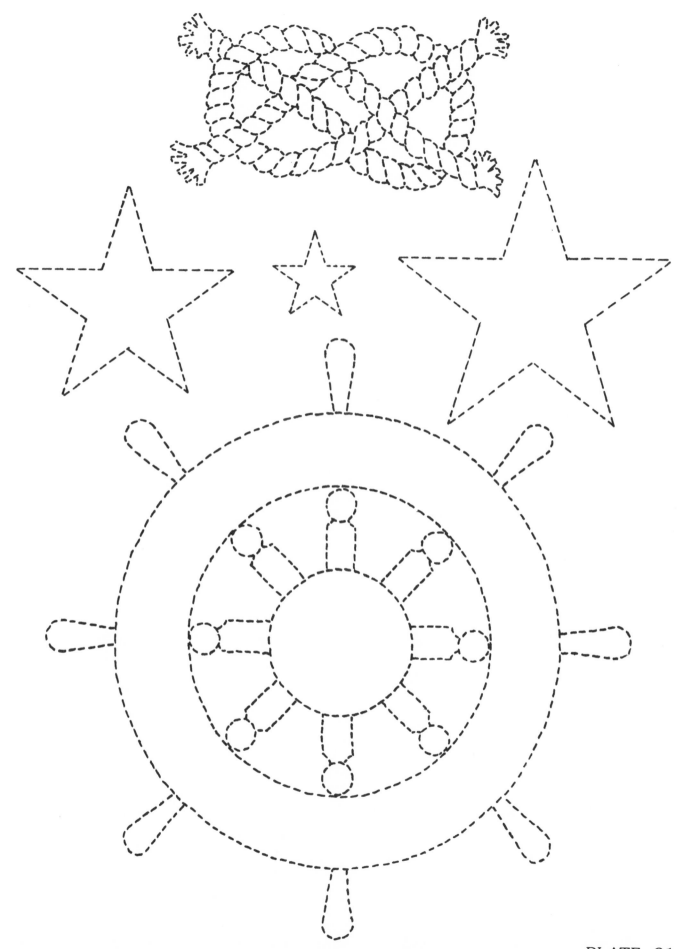

PLATE 21

PLATE 22

PLATE 23

PLATE 24

PLATE 25

PLATE 26

PLATE 27

PLATE 28

PLATE 29

PLATE 30

PLATE 31

PLATE 32